W9-AQV-639

Date: 2/1/12

J 598.47 LAN
Landau, Elaine.
Emperor penguins : animals of
the snow and ice /

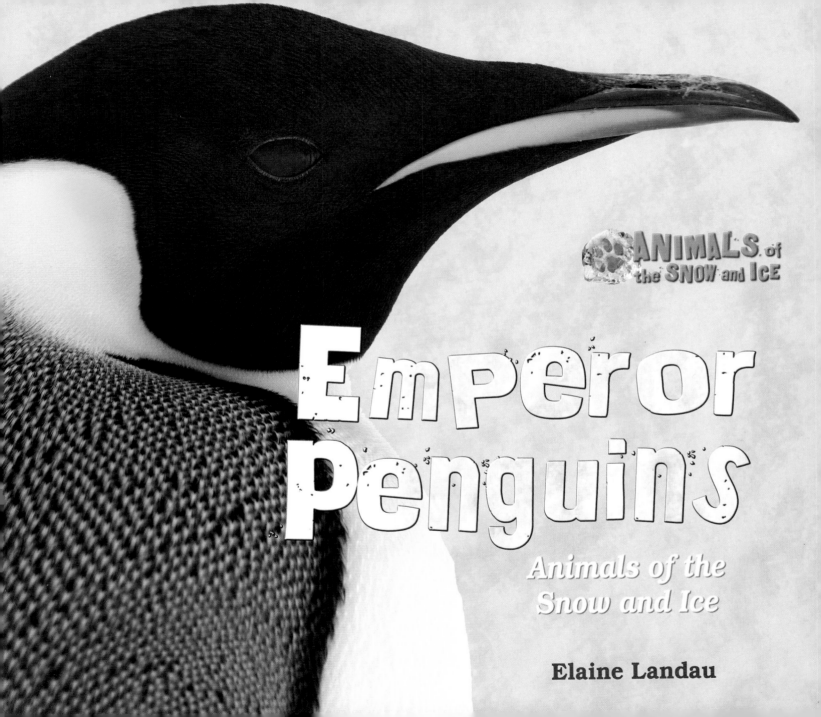

ANIMALS of the SNOW and ICE

Emperor Penguins

Animals of the
Snow and Ice

Elaine Landau

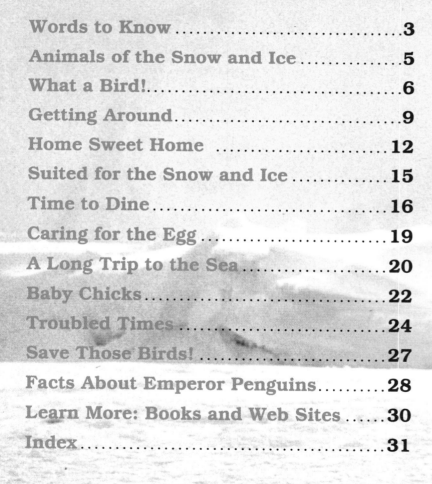

Contents

Words to Know

Antarctica—The large frozen land around the South Pole.

brood pouch—A gap in the feathers of most birds that covers their egg or eggs.

crèche (kresh)—A group of penguin chicks.

down—A bird's soft, fluffy feathers. They are often under the top layer of feathers.

global warming—A rise in the average temperature of Earth's surface. This warming causes climate change.

prey—To hunt another animal for food; an animal that is hunted to be eaten.

regurgitate (ree GUR jih tayt)—To spit up food from the stomach back into the mouth.

Penguins cannot fly, but they are very good divers and swimmers.

Animals of the Snow and Ice

Can you guess the bird I am thinking of? This bird cannot fly. Its body is too heavy and its wings are too small. However, this bird is a good swimmer. It needs to be. It lives in the ocean and on the sea ice off the coast of Antarctica. Its home is one of the coldest and windiest places on Earth.

The special bird I am thinking of is the emperor penguin. It is the world's biggest penguin. It is also the only one that can survive Antarctica's very cold winters. It is a true animal of the snow and ice.

ANTARCTICA
(south pole)

What a Bird!

Emperor penguins are large birds that waddle on two feet. They can grow up to a little more than three feet tall and weigh between 50 and 80 pounds. Some may weigh more than you!

These birds look like they are wearing tuxedos. They have dark feathers on their heads and backs and white feathers on their bellies.

Yet they have some color, too. Their short, thick necks are blue-gray. There are patches of yellow feathers behind their eyes. A bit more yellow and orange is on their chests and beaks.

The male and female birds look alike. They are the same size and have the same coloring. If you see them on the ice, you cannot tell them apart.

Emperor penguins can be more than three feet tall and weigh up to eighty pounds.

Getting Around

Emperor penguins are super swimmers. They can dive deeper than any other bird in the world. They can stay under the water for about twenty minutes. Few humans can come close to doing that.

These birds are built for swimming. They have webbed feet, and their wings act as flippers. Their average swimming speed is about six miles per hour. That is faster than the fastest human swimmer.

Emperor penguins can dive deeper than any other bird in the world. They can stay underwater for up to twenty minutes.

These birds are slow walkers, though. They waddle around on the ice. But they can move faster if they want to! They flop down on their bellies and use their wings to push their bodies across the ice. They can travel as far as fifty miles on their bellies to get to the ocean.

Since penguins walk very slowly, they sometimes slide on their bellies to go faster!

Home Sweet Home

Emperor penguins live in Antarctica, the bitterly cold land that covers the South Pole. Antarctica is surrounded by water. These penguins live in the chilly waters and on the sea ice. The sea ice is frozen solid and attached to the land. So some emperor penguins never set foot on actual land—only ice!

Temperatures near the South Pole can drop to more than −80 degrees Fahrenheit. Freezing winds blow at high speeds for days. The winter months are the worst. On the coast, most of the animals leave. They return when it is warmer.

Emperor penguins stay there all year, however. They gather together in large groups called colonies. There may be as many as fifty thousand birds in a single colony.

Some penguins never stand on actual land. They walk on ice and swim in water.

Emperor penguins gather in groups to stay warm.

Suited for the Snow and Ice

Emperor penguins are well-suited for life in a very cold place. These birds are not skinny. They have a layer of blubber, or fat, under their skin to keep them warm. Close to their skin, they have a layer of fuzzy down. Both the blubber and the down help keep the birds' body heat in and the cold out.

These birds also have long, waterproof feathers. They overlap to form four thick layers. The feathers are almost like scales. They are covered with an oily coating that keeps out water and wind. Only the strongest winds can ruffle them.

Emperor penguins have other ways to keep warm. They tip their feet up and under their feathers. This puts their body weight on their heels and tails so that less of their feet touch the cold ice.

Since emperor penguins like to stay together, they are able to beat the cold. These birds huddle in a close group. They often move from the outside to the inside of the huddle where it is warmer.

Time to Dine

Adult emperor penguins are very good hunters. They hunt for food in the icy ocean where they live. They dive into the ocean to catch fish, squid, and shrimplike animals called krill.

Leopard seals hunt penguins, and they may eat more than one a day.

These birds hunt, but they are also hunted. Leopard seals prey on them. The seals hunt both the young and older emperor penguins because they are easier to catch. Large seabirds, such as the southern giant petrel, prey on young emperor penguin chicks. Up to one third of chick deaths are from petrel attacks.

A male penguin balances his egg on his feet so it doesn't freeze on the ice.

Caring for the Egg

Every March, pairs of emperor penguins mate. By about mid-April to June, the female lays just one egg. She carefully passes the egg to her male partner to care for. He will keep the egg with him for about 65 days.

The male bird holds the egg on his feet. He tucks it under a thick fold in his skin. This skin is called a brood pouch. The egg stays warm there.

The males in the colony all huddle together in a large group to stay warm on the ice. They do not leave the colony.

A Long Trip to the Sea

As soon as they pass their eggs to the males, the females start their long trip to the sea. They waddle and slide for up to fifty miles. When they reach the sea, they eat and eat and eat.

The females do not return to the colony until July or August. Then the males pass the eggs or recently hatched chicks back to them. Now the males go to the sea. It is finally their turn for a meal. Since they do not leave the colony while they are caring for the eggs, they have not eaten for more than 100 days!

3 to 50 miles
march to rookery
APRIL

Females
go off to feed

Mating
MAY

Females return

Males go feed;
Cycle repeats
6 more times

Adults leave;
Chicks fledge;
Ice breaks up
DEC

Males incubate eggs
JUNE-JULY

Hatching
AUGUST

Feeding chicks
SEPT-OCT

Chicks form groups
to stay warm
OCT-NOV

21

Baby Chicks

Surprise! Newly hatched emperor penguins are not black and white. Instead, they have a thin coat of gray down. Over time, it grows to a thick, fluffy cover.

A new chick stays covered by its mother's brood pouch for about three weeks. During this time, the chick's mother feeds it. She spits up, or regurgitates, food she ate at sea.

The mother and father penguins take turns going back and forth to the sea. They eat and bring back food for their chicks. The chicks stay behind in groups called crèches.

There are many chicks in these groups. Yet the parents still find their own chicks when they come back from the sea. Both the parents and the chicks know each other by their call.

As the weather warms in January, the ice breaks up. This brings the sea closer to the young birds. By then, they can take care of themselves. They leap into the sea to feed for the first time when they are about six months old.

Penguin chicks stay behind in groups while their parents go to sea to hunt.

Troubled Times

The emperor penguin may be in trouble. No one knows exactly how many emperor penguins there are today. In the 1970s, scientists saw the number of emperor penguins drop. At that point, there were only about half as many penguins as there had been in the past.

Now, global warming may become a threat to the penguins. As temperatures rise, the sea ice melts. When this happens, the emperor penguins' nesting sites disappear. The birds are pushed into smaller areas.

Warmer temperatures can also be especially hard on the young chicks. The thinner ice breaks up more easily. It is swept out to sea by strong winds. At times, young chicks have been blown away before they were ready to survive on their own.

25

Save Those Birds!

Some people are trying to help. They have asked businesses and elected leaders to find ways to lessen global warming.

The Antarctica Treaty has been signed by forty-six nations. This agreement protects the area. It bans mining for oil and gas. It also stops armies from testing war weapons there. If mining and weapons testing were allowed, new roads, airfields, and ports would have to be built. This would harm the emperor penguins' homes.

The Antarctica Treaty helps the birds, too. It makes it illegal to harm penguins. It is also against the law to take their eggs.

We should all care about what happens to these special birds. Humans have made their lives harder. Now it is up to us to help them. The world would not be the same without the emperor penguin.

Facts About Emperor Penguins

❆ The emperor penguin's long march to the sea can be up to fifty miles each way.

❆ Only one out of five emperor penguin chicks survives its first year of life.

❆ While guarding their eggs, males may lose as much as one third of their body weight. They do not go to sea to feed until the females return from the sea after several months.

❆ If a newly hatched chick fell off its parent's feet and onto the ice, it would die of the cold in less than two minutes.

❆ It can be more than thirty degrees warmer in the center of a penguin huddle than on the outside.

Learn More

Books

Bredeson, Carmen. *Emperor Penguins Up Close*. Berkeley Heights, N.J.: Enslow Publishers, Inc., 2006.

Kalman, Bobbie. *The Life Cycle of an Emperor Penguin*. New York: Crabtree Publishing, 2006.

Squire, Ann O. *Penguins*. New York: Children's Press, 2007.

Trattles, Patricia. *Emperor Penguins*. Minneapolis: Lerner Publishing, 2006.

Web Sites

KidZone Penguin Facts.
<http://www.kidzone.ws/animals/penguins/facts10.htm>

Penguin Facts & Fun.
<http://www.penguinscience.com>

Index

A

Antarctica, 5, 12, 27
Antarctica Treaty, 27

B

bellies, 10
blubber, 15
brood pouch,19, 22

C

chick, 17, 20, 22, 24
colony, 12, 19, 20
crèche, 22

D

down, 15, 22
diving, 9, 16

E

egg, 19, 20, 27

emperor penguin
   appearance, 6
   habitat, 5
   height, 6
   weight, 6

F

feathers, 6, 15
feet, 6, 9, 15, 19
food, 16, 20, 22
   fish, 16
   krill, 16
   squid, 16

G

global warming, 24, 27

L

leopard seal, 17

M

mating, 19

N

nesting site, 24

P

prey, 17

R

regurgitate, 22

S

sea ice, 5, 12, 24
southern giant petrel, 17
South Pole, 12
staying warm, 15, 19
swimming, 5, 9

T

trip to sea, 20, 22

W

waddle, 6, 10, 20
wings, 5, 9, 10

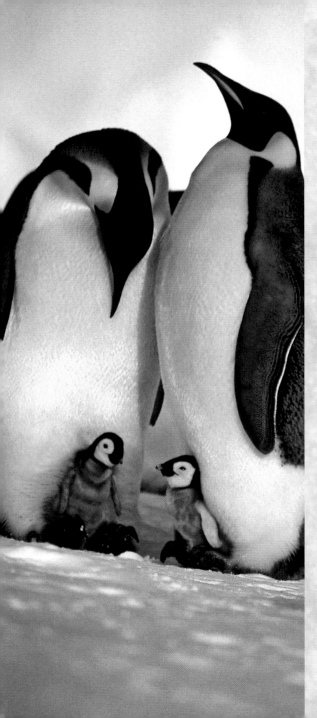

Enslow Elementary, an imprint of Enslow Publishers, Inc.
Enslow Elementary® is a registered trademark of Enslow Publishers, Inc.

Library of Congress Cataloging-in-Publication Data

Landau, Elaine.
    Emperor penguins : animals of the snow and ice / Elaine Landau.
        p. cm. — (Animals of the snow and ice)
    Includes bibliographical references and index.
    Summary: "Provides information for young readers about emperor penguins, including habitat,
eating habits, mating, babies, and conservation"—Provided by publisher.
    ISBN 978-0-7660-3462-4
    1. Emperor penguin—Juvenile literature. I. Title.
    QL696.S473L35 2011
    598.47—dc22

                                        2009006479

Printed in the United States of America

092009 Lake Book Manufacturing, Inc., Melrose Park, IL

10 9 8 7 6 5 4 3 2 1

Photo Credits: © 1999, Artville, LLC, p. 5 (map); © 2009 Jupiterimages Corporation, p. 32; Bryan
& Cherry Alexander/Photo Researchers, Inc., pp. 2–3; © Doug Allan/naturepl.com, p. 8; © Fred
Olivier/naturepl.com, p. 18; Fritz Polking/Visuals Unlimited, Inc., p. 29; © Graham Robertson/ardea.
com, p. 14; © Graham Yuile/iStockphoto.com, p. 1; © Ingo Arndt/Minden Pictures, p. 7; © Jan
Vermeer/Foto Natura/Minden Pictures, pp. 16–17, 23; © Keith Szafranski/iStockphoto.com, p. 26;
© M. Watson/ardea.com, p. 13; Photographer's Choice/Getty Images, pp. 10–11; Riser/Getty Images,
pp. 24–25; The Image Bank/Getty Images, pp. 4–5, 30; Zina Deretsky, National Science Foundation,
p. 21.

Cover Photo: © Graham Yuile/iStockphoto.com

Enslow Elementary
an imprint of

E Enslow Publishers, Inc.
40 Industrial Road
Box 398
Berkeley Heights, NJ 07922
USA

http://www.enslow.com